I0459636

Advance Praise for The Unheard Music:

"You can't go wrong with Dan Wright's latest collection, The Unheard Music. I enjoyed so many things in this book, from the tight, compact muscularity of 'Video Game Rental' to the dark and sharp 'I Hope Whoever Took My Anti-Depressants Is Happy Now' to what might possibly be my favorite of all, 'Ain't It Just Like Norman Fucking Rockwell.' These poems deserve to be heard, so do yourself a favor and have a listen."

-John Burroughs, author of *Rattle and Numb* and 2022-23 U.S. Beat Poet Laureate

"Daniel W. Wright embraces a rock n' roll ethos, which shines through in his poetic stylings. He weaves together reflections on the social landscape, pop culture, the joys of friendship, and absurdity of everyday life, creating a colorful window into his unique world."

-Kyle Brandt-Lubart, co-author of *It Made a Sound*

Works by Daniel W. Wright:

The Unheard Music

A Ludicrous Split 3 [with Gabriel Ricard & Kevin Ridgeway]

Snake Oil

Call Center

Tonight's Main Event [with Gabriel Ricard]

From Obscurity to Oblivion: Collected Poems 2008-2017

Love Letters from the Underground

Brian Epstein Died for You

Rodeo of the Soul

The Unheard Music

Poems by Daniel W. Wright

Kung Fu Treachery Press
Rancho Cucamonga, CA

Copyright © Daniel W. Wright, 2024

First Edition: 1 3 5 7 9 10 8 6 4 2

ISBN: 978-1-958182-99-4

LCCN: 2024952301

Cover image: Jim McGowin

Title page image: Josh Basco

Author photo: Caitlin McKenna

All rights reserved. No part of this publication may be
reproduced or transmitted in any form or by any means,
electronic or mechanical, including photocopying,
recording or by info retrieval system, without prior
written permission from the author.

Acknowledgments

Some of these poems previously appeared in *The Literary Parrot, 365 Days: A Poetry Anthology Volume 3, 365 Days: A Poetry Anthology Volume 4, The Notes Will Carry Me Home*, and *Book of Matches*

To Gabriel Ricard and Kevin Ridgeway, thanks for being the Chico and Harpo to my Groucho.

To Jesse Eikmann, Denmark Laine, and Cierra Lowe, I couldn't have run Back of the Class without you!

To RC Patterson, thank you for always keeping it zen.

To Dunaway Books, thank you for always being a second home and second family to me.

To CBGB, thanks for being the best dive bar in South City.

To Alex, James, Ian, Mary, and everyone else at Exhibit B, much love! Keep the poetry flame alive in Chicago!

To Damian Rucci and the New Jersey Poetry Renaissance, keep fighting that good fight on the coast!

To Charlie Getter and the rest of the crew at 16th and Mission, save a spot for me. I'll be there soon!

To you, who have purchased this book, thank you! Enjoy!

Table of Contents:

This book is dedicated to Elise Giammanco
Thank you for never letting me give up

"Imagine a world where art
is the only motivation."

- Rob Tyner

The Unheard Music

Four Star Night

Today's paradise is tomorrow's wasteland
"You're so talented I hate you"
are the best words an artist
hopes to hear
Whiskey dick writers
with no ink in their pens
caught between a cuddle and showtime
feel like Steve Urkel
about to step in the ring
with Mike Tyson
Paranoid societies open for business
when people can't be satiated
by the usual noise

Lovers leap only safe distances
after checking out
a potential partner's credit report
The most talented people I've ever met
are the most lazy
Geniuses with an excuse

Never settling means a long time of loneliness
Salvation army trombone
plays in a one-man parade
Cats allowed to kill
whatever they can catch
and prance around with it
in their mouths
Different data means different results

Everyone now has a different reality
Hard to see the forest and the trees
I just want the real reality
to raise its hand

Long term grudges cripple the soul
So many walk around
with a war in their head
Evil falls in line
Good commits friendly fire
because the word came down
with no evidence
that there was a traitor in the camp
Last train for Tucson takes opportunity away
Sleepless in St. Louis
longs for long distance love
Who knows who takes what seriously anymore
The see-saw goes up and down
both sides fear the result

Walking on the ceiling for a bit
to catch your bearings
Fallouts with old friends
call you to arms
Make you move to Switzerland
Friday nights plead the fifth
for a fistful of dollars
Masks slowly removed
with all the stage presence
you can muster
It's showtime, folks
Never let them see you bleed

#instapoets

I thought
as poets
our job was to dig deep
to discuss the universal truths
in a way
no one else dares to

But all I see
so far
is a bunch of people
trying to get jobs
writing Hallmark gift cards

Don't Move, Don't Move, Don't Move

All notions to be a hero
leave the body
when that semi-automatic
points in your direction
with wallet and phone
gently lifted
from pockets

The one who spoke
spoke gently
Talking in the same timbre
one does to a child
when trying to pull a splinter

When it was done
they walked away
like nothing had happened
As though those tense few seconds
were an anomaly
Something experienced
outside of normal time and space
though the results
felt pretty fucking final

The only thing I was truly scared of
was their potential anger
when the realization hit
that they had robbed someone
as broke

as I am
That they might've shot me
out of spite

Thankfully
my record of never taking a bullet
remained intact
I almost wanted to be there
when they saw
the one dollar in my wallet
and a phone that was already dead
with a cracked screen
Maybe next time
they'll try a little harder
and go after someone
who isn't one bad day
from where they are

In Paris, You Can Still See One Hundred Years Ago

Wind blows in the Paris underground
as a woman sings opera from her window
The Spanish quarter at dawn
feels like somewhere out of time
A man asks me for a cigarette
Inexplicably, I have one
and light it with a zippo
a barfly had loaned me
the night before
but I was too caught up in the moment
to remember to give it back

Show Me on the Doll Where This
Book Hurt You

They finally started coming for the information
Just as they once went after music
Put a parental warning sticker over my mouth
and the mouth
of every writer out there
To Kill a Mockingbird and *Lady Chatterly's Lover*
are cast back in the fire
Howl and *Tropic of Cancer* are back in court
The busybodies are out for blood
out for ink
and out after all the silly misfits

Evil deeds have hidden behind
noble language so long
they are now transparent
But now it stands
with the possibility of every Missouri librarian
facing anything
from a $500 fine
to a year behind bars
No one has that kinda money
or that kinda time

It all comes down to small people
wanting big power
Maybe the biggest of all
The power to control the mind

To limit what goes in
Because these parents already have
their kids' lives mapped out
And know who they want
living in their neighborhoods
A perfect little life all planned out
And there's no room in a perfect little life
for questioning all the little plans

Lois Lane Never Loved Superman

Don't call it love
ace reporter Lois Lane
Until you notice
how he cuts his fingernails
Until you smell the cologne
mixed with his natural musk
Until you see the mistakes
he made in how he shaved that day

Until you notice his shy smile
that belies a concealed confidence
Until you see past a pair of glasses,
a slight slouch,
and perfectly combed hair
that can miraculously produce a spit curl
on cue
Until you notice such details,
don't call it love
Love actually notices these kinds of things

A Whole Lot of Nothing

Whenever I see a familiar face
it is inescapable
that we will ask about
what the other has done
since we last saw each other
Nine times out of ten
the other person will say,
"Nothing."

It always strikes me as odd
that people give
"Nothing"
as an answer so often
and my mind
will always focus on that
as the conversation progresses
I'll imagine this person
just sitting at a table
when they're not at a job or going to bed
contently staring at a wall
If I know they have a partner
and/or kids
I'll imagine them staring at the wall as well
with one of them saying
"Y'know, this really is a nice wall to stare at."

If I haven't seen the person in years
I'll even start to think that that wall
might have something to it

if it was worth being stared at
for years
I'll wonder if I caught them
the one time
they decided to not stare at wall
That they had thought to themselves
earlier in the day
"You know what,
maybe there's more to life
than this wall!"
But before they go out
they'll pet the wall
to let it know that their going out
is no reflection on the wall

It always makes me wonder
what they consider to be newsworthy
To me, everything is newsworthy
Having a family is newsworthy
A good job is newsworthy
and I say brag about it
Especially if I haven't seen you
in forever
But to them, nothing ever is special
Even if I know they traveled Europe
for a whole summer
If they performed brain surgery
for the first time
or if they found the secret of eternal life
They would only mention it
if someone else brought it up
by saying something
along the lines of "Yeah, that was a thing."

When the catching up is over,
the pressure of getting on with our day
will get the better
of the both of us
and this familiar face and I
will both make declarations
that we need to catch up soon
that neither of us
will want to follow up on
As the truth of it is
both of us
would be so much happier
sitting at home
doing a whole lot of nothing

Slacker Kids and Forever Dreams
in the Valley of Flowers

Sitting on the same hill
that I watched so many sunsets
in my youth
remembering that the sunsets of 1996
seemed a little more special
than the sunsets of today

Recalling the thrill of waking up every day
just to call your friends
Ride your bikes on pleasant valley Sundays
Saturday's kids who now had the whole week
Definitions never done
now an afterthought
Digging in the couch for dimes for Vess sodas
Half to drink
Half to shake and see explode
after throwing them from the top
of a concrete stairwell
Maybe get a DQ sundae
if there was enough change
in the couch

Making up stories
to see if anyone would believe them
Risking life and limb to prove yourself
Too old to play but never too old for trouble
Journeying through cancer ridden creeks
and waterways

because we felt special
for discovering a shortcut
we really shouldn't have taken

Dirty jokes and gag gifts at L&L
Not sure if we ever got them
but we told them anyway
Always remembering the blonde jokes
Dad would tell
Feeling like George Carlin
when you told them to friends

Borrowing newspapers on lawns
not yet taken inside
to use as goal posts
to play hockey in the street
Life was timeless
Days were new
The world was an oyster
now it's a clam

Lives get lived
Friends may part
But for one glorious summer
we lived true
Hand to heart

Letting a SpamBot Down Gently

Please don't take it personally
but I just don't believe you're real
I'm sure the webcam
you asked me to check out
is nice
but if I wanted
to get my rocks off
bad enough
there are endless porn sites
I could go to
that are free

I have to ask
what was it
that gave the skin of the model
in your profile pic
that nice sheen?
Was it tanning butter?
Perhaps a nice salad dressing?
It would've been nice
if you would have been real
or
on the off chance
you are real
lived in this country

But as we have no friends in common
As we have never met
and as you have no vowels

in your name
I had to err
on the side of caution
and decline your friend request

Do not despair though
I think I might be able
to help you find someone
who is more your speed
There's an African prince
who sent me an e-mail a little while ago
His throne has been usurped
and word is
he's worth billions
and willing to reward anyone
who dares help him fund
his revolution
to reclaim his rightful place
on the throne
Something tells me
the two of you
would hit it off
just fine

And This Poet You Cannot Change

It may not be much
but an indignity
that poets never have to endure
is being asked to play
"Margaritaville"
or "Freebird"

Encouraging My Friend's Hatred of Morrissey

Over a couple of beers
my friend and I talked
about how much
we used to love The Smiths
but now would not touch Morrissey
for as far as we could throw
his vegan ass

"I want to be the shoe that hit
George W. Bush in the face
except be the pork steak
that hits Morrissey
in the fucking face
because fuck Morrissey!"
My friend said as he finished off
another High Life

We talked of Johnny Marr
being the only saving grace of the band
How the demands of Morrissey
forced Marr to be a makeshift manager
as no other manager
could deal with Morrissey's diva demands
and how that led
amongst other things
to Marr quitting the band
And how Morrissey still resents Marr so much
he has said he won't perform
in the state of Oregon

simply because of a rumor
that Johnny Marr lives in Portland

We talked of Morrissey's high demands
whenever he came to a venue
How there must be a team
to cater to his every whim
and how
as talented as his backing band
may be
none of them
can still figure out
how to properly do
the intro
to "This Charming Man"

And that was all before
we talked about his politics

Leanan Sídhe

The fairy dances in the field
Helplessly hoping for a someone
to dance with her
Not to own her like property
Not to capture her
as though she were a lightning bug
But to dance in morning dew
after an early storm
and the Lovefool only watches from a distance
admiring her grace

She has been called trickster
She has been called harlequin
Her song is the unheard music
She may disappear in a forest
to leave a triquetra
letting you know she was there
She is sky
She is earth
She is water
She was once
a Gaelic goddess

She can stroll upon water
as blue as her eyes
Her name is Beloved
though if the mood strikes
she may claim to be Danu

Visits in dreams
can make one fortify themself
She has been there before
but only once
did the Lovefool make it transparent
and she vanished
though her footsteps
have been in every book
since he first saw her

To utter a word
no matter how far away
would be a banshee's scream
to Mother Earth
who would let the fairy know
that she was on his mind
and again
the fairy would disappear

So that is why the Lovefool sits
admiring her dance from a distance
because nothing in this world
worthwhile
can be forced to do anything
Though he longs to dance with her
it is only when
she wants to dance with you
that you both can enjoy

Kafka

Someone recently told me
that they could tell
from the kind of stuff
I write
that I've read
a lot of Kafka.
I actually haven't.
It just so happens
on some days,
I am the insect.

My Father's Poems

While looking through boxes
my mother had left me
I found a piece of paper
with typewritten poems
my father had written

One carried on
about Taster's Choice coffee
and 1980s consumerism
Another was about a fly in a grocery store
shitting on the produce

Far be it from me
to ever critique
the writing
of another poet
but since he abandoned
my Mom and I
I take pleasure
in knowing
I'm definitely the better writer

That may be petty
but it doesn't make it
any less true

Sigma

The man sat at the table
with his friends
explaining that he
was a

SIGMA MALE

And that a

SIGMA MALE

was outside the bounds
of the hierarchy
and did his own thing
and thus
was just as sexually attractive
to women
as an **ALPHA MALE**

I don't know
where people pull this shit from
but once upon a time
there was another term
for guys like this

ASSHOLE

And it still seems
more fitting

Rimbaud's Vertebrae (Or How the Hipster was Born)

Rimbaud decided
to surgically remove
a piece of his vertebrae
so he could suck his own dick
But he kept that piece of himself
in a jar
And he named it Paul Verlaine
because it was the only reason
he was ever able
to get off

Elegy for Neeli

While at work one day
I heard my phone ringing.
I looked down and saw
Neeli Cherkovski was calling me.
I had been fortunate enough
to meet him
over the summer
I had sent him a message on Facebook
letting him know how much of an influence
he had been.
He responded
"Send poems."
And I was too scared to do so
Four days later he sent another message
"Send poems now"
So I did.
He said he liked them.
You could have knocked me over
with a feather
after I read that.

When I went out to San Francisco that summer,
I had asked him
if he would like to get coffee and hang out.
He responded that he would love to.
But rather than going out,
he invited me over to his house.
We drank coffee and talked poetry.

I let him know how much his work
meant to me
How his book
Whitman's Wild Children
had set me on my path as a writer
and had helped me find my tribe.
The day was great
and I even got to sit in
on him teaching a class
over Zoom.
But I never expected
to get a call from him
months later.

When I answered he asked, "Is this Ned?"
"No, this is Dan."
"Who?"
"Dan."
"Oh, hey man! How's it going?"

We talked for twenty minutes
about our favorite poets
and the craft of poetry.
He sounded excited
when I mentioned
Jack Hirschman and Bob Kaufman.
The last thing he said
before we hung up
was, "Keep up the good work, man!
Hope to see you out here again."

I thought about reaching out
the next time I was in San Francisco.
But despite everything,
my damn imposter syndrome
got the best of me.
By the time I realized
how silly that was
it was too late.

All that's left to say
is how grateful I am
that a poet I looked up to for so long,
who had known
some of the greatest poetic minds
of a generation,
showed me a kindness
that even as an adult
I'm not used to
when
by all rights
he didn't have to.

Thank you, Neeli.

Porch Pirates

I came home
to find a package
waiting at my door
The address said it was from Germany
It was a Bukowski tribute
that I had contributed to
that featured
a whole host of poets
much better than myself
who I was proud
to share pages with

When I grabbed the package
I noticed one side
had already been slit open
I looked inside
and thankfully the book was there
I guess porch pirates don't care for poetry

All My Friends are Turning Forty

I knew it'd happen eventually
I just thought there was more time
There's always supposed to be more time
but I guess I never learn my lesson
I wonder if that counts as insanity

The back aches a little more
I know I curse, groan, and mumble
every time I have to stand up
I look over at my manager
who is close to retirement age
and still calls me "Kid"
Telling me, "Whatever you do, don't get old!"
as every other Boomer and Gen Xer
seems to relish the fact
that Millennials are getting older
as though we are getting
some karmic justice
and as usual
all we can say is,
"Yeah, and...?"

Still baby-faced but now with graying temples
I wish I could say my youth was fun
And while there were certainly good times
I spent most of it in fear

Fear of consequences that never came
but were always around the corner

Fear of mental illnesses of the past
that tried to hitch a ride
on my brain
as I did my best
to leave them behind
Fear of a self-fulfilling prophecy
given to me
by those who had their own gripes with the world
and wanted to take everyone down with them
because they never lived up to their potential

I can only imagine the fucks not given
as I get older
I actually look forward to it
So many fucks washed away
when I hit 30
If that were any indicator
maybe I'll tell people
what I really think of them
by the time I'm 60

I try to impart what wisdom I can
to my younger friends
hoping the advice can help
in whatever way it can
It may be foolish
but I always have hope
that it can be done
but I find myself biting my lip
whenever I see them
because I always seem compelled to say,
"Whatever you do, don't get older."

A Conversation with a Bee

I passed a bee
walking in the opposite direction from me
as I was coming home
from the store
I made sure not to step on him
and the bee got up on its hind legs
and thanked me for caring enough
to give him enough room
on the sidewalk

I asked him where he was going
and he told me
he was going to find a spot to die
I asked him how he knew
he was going to die
and he told me that he had stung some asshole
who couldn't tell the difference
between him and a yellow jacket
I asked him if he needed a lift
and he said he'd gladly take one

So I put my hand on the ground
and let him crawl on
He asked if he wasn't putting me out
and wanted to make sure
that I didn't have anything
that needed to get in the fridge
I told him to not worry about it

He pointed me
to the direction of a tree
with some nice shade
about half a block up
I asked him if he had any regrets
and he said he didn't have any.
"I've pollinated flowers and got to fuck a Queen.
I've led a pretty good life."
I asked if he wanted me
to stick around.
"That's awful nice," said the bee.
"But we tend to want to die on our own."

I wished the bee well
and he did the same
And I left the bee
Earth's essential worker
to his fate
smiling as he enjoyed
the shade and sun
of a last summer day

I've Heard that Everyone You've Read is More Relevant Than Everyone I've Read

The kids are coming up from behind
Rewriting every Bret Easton Ellis
and Chuck Palahniuk novel
before I ever get a chance to
Coming out of the woodwork
from
New York
and
Los Angeles
Though I still don't know
how they can afford to live
in either city

I'm wondering if I'm already irrelevant
Walking down the street
and seeing too many people
rocking the same look as me
A bunch of Harry Potter hipsters
in blazers and band t-shirts
but who are actually pretty cool
once you get to know them

Walking into a used bookstore
making it known to the store
that they're looking
for an Uncorrected Proof
of A Confederacy of Dunces
Because they want only the good influences

They wanna make something unique
            They all wanna be Tom Robbins
maybe Pynchon
or Hornby
and have bumper stickers on their laptops
            with things like "L.A. is for Quitters"

written on them

            I heard you have a true first edition
        of The Sun Also Rises
  with that extra 'p' in 'stopped'
on Page 181
and maybe a misspell on Page 169
            though you haven't been able to spot it
I heard that you have a collection
  of every Great American Short Story
        that was given to you by a college professor
            who one time had drinks with William Faulkner
            and who was once made uncomfortable
                by being hit on by Allen Ginsberg
                and who thinks he saw Samuel Beckett
but was too scared
to approach him

My mind is ten years behind
every nostalgia obsessed
art-school Brooklynite
Don't believe me?
Just ask them.
            Anything's deep
                if you want it to be

Just look at my social media
Out with the old and in with the ironic

Let's call the world a social construct
and relate it to a fly
that buzzes around a clock
with a light in it
If you don't get it
you ain't learned

No room for the uneducated
in the residencies of the world
         No love for a writer
                 who only has words
                         but no agenda
Is my kind already an endangered species
Where are all the other savages
who would howl at the moon
with me
who have a reason to howl
who could take dead aim
and hit the stars with a bottle

The kids are coming up
from behind
Coming out of the woodwork

                 from the publishers who are always
                         never looking for anybody

Always looking the part
        and always writing that amazing book
                That sells for $30.00 on sale
                        at the nearest convenient
                        overpriced bookstore near you
                        that'll only be worth $6.00
this time next year

The Prettiest Girl in St. Louis

The prettiest girl in St. Louis
has dark hair
and an even darker sense of humor
She could be full of herself
but walks around
full of love
with most passing her by
assuming she is too good
to talk to them
when
in fact
a simple hello
could be the best decision
of your life

She carries herself free
And makes everyone around her
feel invincible
by saying hello
in a way
that makes them feel seen
The prettiest girl in St. Louis
drinks cheap beer
and has been blessed
with good enough genes
to never show an ounce

She can make you feel
confident and insecure

then calm the anxiety
by asking you about your day
The prettiest girl in St. Louis
inspires you to write poems
about the prettiest girl
in St. Louis

Untitled Underlines of a Borrowed Book

Like a friend
pointing out the good bits
when you just wanna watch
the damn movie
Yet still
There's something endearing
even if there are
cursive lines of poetry
so small and off to the side
sometimes better
than the poem
you're reading

They may make you appreciate
a line better
Show you the poetry of a sentence
your brain may have just read
to get to the next one

Like a literary tattoo
that can tell its life story
better than the cracks in the spine
or dog-eared pages
It's important to know
that others know the secrets
a book is about to share
with you

An Up and Coming Neighborhood

Dead bodies
on Dutchtown asphalt
Used car parts lead
to another stolen car
abandoned when the gas ran out
Only thing in the streets
worth a damn
is a Cardinals hat
with a little grease on the brim
still sticky from the Arizona tea
spilled near it
The paint chips off the patio
to show the wooden boards
still wet from the day before

In a few years
none of us will be able
to afford this neighborhood
Maybe they'll finally put some decent transit
up on the North Side
when they move us all up there
While these rundown houses
will be sold
as "original Victorian era architecture
in vibrant urban communities"

Is That Enough to Get the Discount

Some will pay through the nose
just for the satisfaction
of knowing they saved
a few pennies
No matter how much
they actually spent

Just the knowledge
of knowing they paid enough
to get a percentage off
is enough for some
to feel like
they didn't lose
as much as they did
the day before

Digital Love

Together digitally androgynous
Protecting one another
they are two but one
just as much as Aristophanes' speech
on Plato's Symposium

One a little round mirror
with a hole in the middle
because it doesn't mind
being seen through
The other nothing more
than fragile protection
That may not seem like much
but will protect
no matter how the world
chooses to break it
Even on days when where daydreams
scream glitter to the end

One day the two were sold
to a used cd store
with dust in the air
that still smelled of the 1990s
The cd and the jewel case were separated
with the case put out for display
and the cd placed behind the counter
for safekeeping

A few weeks later, a kid came into the store
looking for a five-finger discount on some good music
The kid grabbed the jewel case
cover art intact
And walked past the clerk
with an upper class hyphenated nose
to let the clerk think
he wasn't doing anything wrong
unaware the clerk
was paid too little to care

When the kid saw there was no cd,
he threw the jewel case away
cursing the music store for ripping him off
when all he wanted to do
was steal from them

A few weeks after that
a homeless man found the jewel case
and brought it to the store,
hoping to fool the clerk
into getting a few bucks
It worked
And before the clerk could see
he gave away a few bucks for nothing
his co-worker grabbed the jewel case
and put it back on display

Eventually the cd sold
and the cd and jewel case were reunited
Together digitally androgynous
Because even digital love
deserves a happy ending

Shipwreck

My heart lies in the ninth wave
I wish to speak with the Original Angel
A little can be enough to guide
the transistor voices that lie
in yesterday's newspaper
Some beg to dream of sheep
and some wish to dream big
Some sleep under ice
and some wish they could play nice

The cold weather gripped me by the throat
when I awoke this morning
You can't hide from the world forever
All hibernation and brumation
comes to an end
Epileptic minds beg for a cesarean
Cold feet can lead
to hungry stomachs
Cinematic waves crash
amongst each other
The singular soldier at the mercy
of their imagination

Witch hunts reach
for medieval means to an end
Banshees, mermaids, and lullabies
are fairy tales
Though the stars keep you company
Staring from the sky

Dancing in the sea
Future begs the past
to never give up

Though the fog covers all
except your personal space
You can still see
when a cardinal flies through
Its coat and its song a reminder
that the fog will pass
The cold will pass
and life will always dance again
Just as there is always
the water
Eventually
there will be land

Blowjobs Don't Count

She set fire to everything
And she'll set fire to the remains tonight
All because of a blowjob to a meth addict
who never returned the favor
He wanted her blowjob
because his church going wife
didn't suck dick
And rather than face
the problems of his marriage
that were brought on by him
Including his refusal to get a job
and his many drug addictions
He decided to hit on a woman
he knew was emotionally unstable
but would give him
the endorphin high he required
because she believed in free love
without believing in herself

He never fucked her
because in his church going mind,
he thought he was being a dutiful husband
by
in his words,
"Saving intimacy for his wife"
He led her to believe
he was a friend
And that friends
help each other out

He called her crazy
when the truth came to light
She had been called crazy
 most of her life
All she was
was a rose
with a couple of extra thorns
The church going couple

stayed together
ready to ignore their problems
for another day
And she stands by the fire
ready to do her worst

Give Me Miles

Give me Miles
warts and all
Give me bebop punk jazz
that tells Duke Ellington
to shove it up his ass
A beat that lingers like a car
going for a joyride in a roundabout
That sees the space to move
where others just go ahead

Give me every great album
with a bad pun for a title
that acts as a middle chapter
between the Milestones
That start like a jet engine
and put me in a trance
where I start hitting the typewriter
like a man possessed
The notes and the clacks ringing out
as though the highway of the mind
is begging me to go faster

Give me the veiled insult
to Nancy Reagan
who never knew who he was
when he was being honored that night
by her husband
after he explained again and again
who he was

and why he was there
before relenting and saying,
"It's not like I do anything important
like fuck the President."

Give me the lost projects
that exist in another timeline
The failures
and the fulfillments
Give me every time
a needle hits
the outskirts of a record
when you hear that one pop
before the music starts
Give me all of that
and you shall find freedom
in one beautiful glimpse

Hop on This Dick and Spin, Zuckerberg

Bare ass on the pavement
Desperate eyes
longing for a yes
to anything
Wheelchair row shows the scabs of junkies
that gather like pigeons
looking to collect
any scraps they can
Abandoned shoes look for a new home
in the middle of the street

Scientifically approved female baldness
with decorative scar
makes itself up
to look as pretty as can be
with a red bow
Drugstore cowboy talks
about the last time
they committed suicide
Intellects talk about fascism
like it's their favorite pastime
Fast foods warn they contain cancer
but tell you to put on a mask
before you come in
And the elders wonder
why young folks can't be
as happy as they used to be
when they were young

October 2015

One of my favorite pictures
is of myself and seven friends
with whom I started
this literary journey
We all read at Dunaway Books that night
and had a hell of an after party

I think of how half of this picture
now wants nothing to do with me
One disappeared from all of us
Another I fell out with
over a matter of common sense
One accused me of holding him
and his drug addiction
down in the poetry world
and things never recovered between us
until it was too late

Some found families
others found chaos
I go back to that night in my mind
and laugh at how old
the poems I read that night
now are
They're still good
but they're not who I am anymore
It makes me wonder
if Mick Jagger ever feels silly
singing "Satisfaction"
almost sixty years later.

Wanna Snort Coke in the Iowa Buffet Bathroom?

St. Louis toasts New Jersey
because it's got
just as blue a collar
and just as black
a sense of humor
and also tells a bigger city
to go fuck itself

Cheap beer and '90s tunes
surrounded by regulars
whose skin looks like
weathered catcher's mitts
Who will tell you they love you
if they remember you enough times

Fuck state lines
Your family is wherever love awaits
Be it your hometown
the east
or the west

Truck Stop Cassettes

I miss seeing the big displays
always in the middle
of any truck stop
in America
right passed the snacks
where you'd see a display
of discount cassette tapes
You had to look
for the one name you'd recognize
and it'd be a Greatest Hits Volume 3
with songs you never heard of before

All for a dollar
Re-recorded country classics
done in the style
of your favorite artists
Or instructional tapes
on how to get your eighteen-wheeler
out of the mud

Maybe the comedic stylings
of Ray Stevens
singing a new version of "The Streak"
While the smell
of the truck stop's restaurant
lets you know
someone ordered
the chicken fried steak

Your Blonde Hair is a Northern Star

I feel the longing
to text that I love you
but I can't
A love we both know is there
that never fades
is beautiful and torturous
I will ride out this urge
as I have all the others
I know you know
And that's enough

Everyone as great as you
should have poems
written about them
I'll write as many as I can
because I am forever lost
in your Capricorn kindness

I look at the flights
going to your city
and wish I had the money
One day I will
and we will walk
along the hills
of your city

Video Game Rental

Life is like
a video game rental
Just when you get used
to how things work
your time is up

The Only Argument at Thanksgiving

The only argument at Thanksgiving
came when my aunt's husband
told me he listened
to Joe Rogan
to get all kinds of views
I tried to bite my lip
but couldn't help myself
and blurted out
that I thought Joe Rogan was full of shit

He left the room
and I felt bad
because he's a great guy
and I didn't want to be the cause
of a family fight
the one time a year
I get to see my family

When he came back
he changed topics
and things were good
until he brought it up again
This time I bit my lip better
Joe Rogan was not a hill
worth dying on

Place Post-Modern Quip Here

I was going to leave
a funny one-liner
as a title on this page
And leave the rest blank
but I couldn't think
of a good enough title
to put here

T-Bone

The right of way
doesn't matter
to those who want to be on their way
The car came from nowhere
crashing into the back passenger side door
Then backed up
and sped off
My friend and I came out
relatively unscathed
Our back muscles a little sore
but nothing
a little Advil and Icy Hot couldn't fix

A few more inches to the right
and it would have been
a different story
at least for me
Funny how such a short measurement
can be the difference
between being damn lucky
and a damn shame

When the dust settled
I made a few calls
to those I care about the most
Only one person answered
the one I thought
least likely to answer
A ship that had passed in the night

I'm not much of a religious man
but after the call
I looked up and thanked
whatever guardian angel
was watching over me

Ultra Conservative Outlaw Country

Nothing says you're a rebel
like backing the blue
Supporting a flag
of a country
that didn't last five years
I can think of at least a dozen bands
that have lasted longer
than that

Choosing to not help
your fellow country men and women
does not make you a rebel
It makes you a conceited prick
who doesn't want to do
their part

You wanna talk rebel?
Willie Nelson is a rebel
John Prine was a rebel (R.I.P.)
Kris Kristofferson is a rebel
And they've all gone on record
to say that people who claim to be outlaws
but back crypto fascist authority figures
are dumber than a pile of shit
And that anybody dumb enough
to give money to a man
who has bankrupted
four casinos
deserves to lose their money

My Favorite Song

I tried describing you to someone
but felt embarrassed
when I couldn't find the words
I tried comparing you to a movie star
but no movie star
could come to mind
I tried thinking of a model
but I can't think of the last time
a model ever caught my attention
The only thing I could think of
was the first time I ever heard
my favorite song

It feels like it's always been there
The words never change
but they always relate
to wherever you are in life
No matter how many times in a row
you hear it
it's still somehow never enough
It moves you as much now
as the first time you heard it
and you knew
this song would always be something
you would turn back to
when looking for hope
in those dark days

That's what you are to me

Family Photos

A photo goes
from "That's me"
to "That's my significant other"
to "That's my family member"
to "I think that person was related to us"
to "I don't know who that is"

It's only a matter of time
before we all become
forgotten
so why not live
to be remembered

I've Worked Myself Up from Nothing
to a State of Extreme Poverty

Columbus Street light
and coffee shop days
All too fleeting in inspiration
that calls long distance
from all over world

Folk singers never explain their songs
so why must poets explain their thoughts
Screams of joy and laughter
heard walking uphill both ways
Had to choose
between no cooking and no shitting
when apartment hunting

Thought I was lost for a second
Read a good book
It put me right
The right kind of art
is a rainbow Molotov cocktail
exploding colors in your mind

So many want free love
but are scared shitless when they get it
Traveled all over the world
to read my work to strangers
It gets me pats on the back
and a few free drinks
But at the end of the day

I still feel like a memorable stranger
who should change their name
to That Guy

Fuck mid-20th century standards
for success
They still mess
with anyone
trying to make a living
by following a passion
No longer applicable in this day and age
Though still wonder
if I can make it
as a New York Times bestseller
It's still valid if I can make it
but if not
it's outdated

Space of living
way smaller
but more freedom
The tightwire is tighter
The net is removed
Giving trust to a trust fall
too high for me
to have ever taken before

Make the Pass

I ask every young person I meet
to be better
than my generation
Be the Nirvana
to our Pixies
Tear the fascists down
The fight is never over
the sword is just passed along
one generation to the next
but that doesn't mean the older generation
has to stop their part
in fighting the good fight

Gracey

She collected her farts in a jar
and her menstrual blood in glass vials
She sold them over the internet
to anybody who would have them
and sold out of the first batch
Gotta respect the hustle

Indirect Wheels, April 13th

Magic is the color of the curtains
that blow in dreams
of the blindfolded piano
trying to feel a comfortable next step
The perfect end of a star
looking for a light
The education that comes
from a love poem written well

Mourn the Wolf King

At the twilight of the Baba Gods
the moon felt its first footsteps
and the Hell's Angels beat Altamont
into embarrassment
Tarantino heroes weren't there
to stop reality from giving us
an ending we didn't deserve

Those who remain
mourn the messages of the Wolf King
Blind eyes turned towards his love for family
Topanga Canyon rings hallow
when no one believes
in the awakening

Summer ends when the water is tapped
The genius plays one last song on his piano
While the archeologists excavate
for lost messages of the Wolf King
but all they find is his top hat

You Had One Job

I saw a book for sale
an autobiography
of Tupac Shakur's
personal bodyguard
I don't think he was very good
at his job

Sleight of Hand

Chasing a magician
because you believe the world
to be magic
It's not my place to tell you
there is no Santa Claus
but I don't want you to fly too far
on the ground

Sanitariums for the rich
when they don't want to talk
about a problem
The faithless brag about scams
they think they scammed
and will get more rich
than the rest

Scars from childhood
that a certain kind regard
as disfiguring
and others regard as life
Empty speeches are believed
because they sound like dreams
Centering chi
in a house you don't live in
because you believe
it is your destiny
to do so

Some are destined to be gilded birds
in a plastic cage
Some have packages too pretty
to be taken seriously
Some see beyond and want magic
when they forget that results are still needed
And when all of the above
comes together
most don't know what to do

so they walk away
because to believe in a falling star
is a failure
too many don't want to go through
again

We Built This City…

It's not that good a song
in fact some say it was the worst thing
ever connected
to Jefferson Airplane
Some have speculated
that when Grace Slick recorded this
there was as much coke in her system
as there was Aquanet in her hair

But hearing it always makes me smile
because it's just the right amount
of 1980s cheese
I think about the year it came out
and the possibilities for so many
The fallen who were still alive
who all looked at 2020
as a Jetsons-esque future

Times were tough
but they weren't worse
Like songs good or bad
it remains a little pocket to the past
Where one can contemplate eternity
with an indifference towards Heaven

An Atlantic City of the Mind

There's a darkness on the edge
of every building
priced to stand vacant
just enough to be an overcast of the soul
of those who walk by
and wonder where the sun went
The casino stands on the grave
of the last chance many had
No one mourns when a city dies
people just leave
because it's not fun anymore
while those with no choice
but to stay
get on a soapbox
to discuss plans
that will never follow through

I know I shouldn't be smoking again
but I've gone so long
without one
I can quit whenever I want
and sometimes a vice or two or three
or four or five
in a city built on beer
is the only balm
that can soothe a bad day

Leaning against a brick wall
on a smoke break from my day off
like a Springsteen working class hero
wanting to pick a fight
with every Bon Jovi hipster fuck you see
whose good looks hide
how well they can throw hands
Smelling home in the streets when it rains
Walking past spray painted "Yo Mama" jokes
on the side of a back alley garage

If Chicago is the New York of the Midwest
Then St. Louis is its Jersey
Half-forgotten and underrated
A beautiful garden with wildflowers
surrounded by well-mannered walls
where you learn hard truths
through hard times
and an offer to smoke with someone
is a reminder
that it's going to be okay

The More Things Change

I think about the possibility of dying alone
like my grandfather
From bronchitis
or some other illness
that could have easily been treated
if caught in time
I worry of dying friendless
in an apartment
Undiscovered for at least a week
With no one to tell my story
I have tried to live to the fullest
because no friends stay

I worry about the monster
that sits deep inside
that I try to starve as much as I can
because I'm afraid of the worst person
I could ever become
Because I have seen the results
of those who came before me
I have heard the stories
A century and some change
isn't that long
when you overthink about it

The physical abuse my grandfather
inflicted on my grandmother
The abandonment my father left
at my mother's door

And the verbal abuse my stepfather screamed
upon anyone in his line of sight
who he knew would never fight back
The alcoholism of every man
who felt deep down
they were never good enough
And the chip on my shoulder
that wants to blow up
every bridge of love
someone builds towards me

I worry I'm just as much a coward
as those who came before me
because I don't want to face this
But I know I have to
Cycles only break
when you face the greatest fear

I Hope Whoever Took My Anti-Depressants
Is Happy Now

Let's sink to the bottom of the lake
to get a new perspective
I can tell from how you drink
that you got a bright future in sales
Move from the Midwest
to the Mid-South
to the Northeast
to the Pacific Northwest
to realize what the problem was all along
Catching yourself in catching up
with an old friend
turning conversation into a bitchfest
and trying to steer things
in a positive direction
if you knew where that was

Forgetting more names
because when you meet enough people
faces and body types all blend together
Showing six forms of ID
to your nearest authority figure
to be rejected for a raise in status
Offering to be rude to speak truth to power
lets you keep a pride
that can't pay the bills
Kindness of opposite genders
viewed as unrequited love
by those who have seen too many movies

because overtures are only said
by those who overstate

Finding new ways to say
the same five things
we've said
since we were handed
our diploma
Overstating the intelligence of others
by calling them a genius
when in fact
they're just smart enough
to not be dumb
and overthinking about how
the bedsheets and pillows
won't let them sleep

The Stench of Death on the Youngest of Us

The hole in his cheek grows bigger
as he walks around in a hooded cloak
looking like the spirit
who is on stand-by
waiting to collect

Outliving everyone's expectations
and disappearing for long periods
that no one knows
what has become of him

My mind turns to morbid thoughts
wondering if any of us will get the news
when he does pass
or if we'll have to hold
a private vigil
long after he is laid to rest
so we can have a chance
to mourn a friend

When They Drop That Needle Down

(A Poem for Bobby Stevens)

I can't count the times
I've put the record on my turntable
But still
after all this time
that first song
gives me goosebumps

To take every nostalgic bone
in one's body
and make them yearn
is a talent like no other
I always think of the words of your song
whenever I place a record
on the turntable

The smallest and simplest ways
to see the world
bring you back to center
And make you face
evolutions in a heavy present
In that way
poets are always a friend
because if a friend can't tell you
the straight truths of the world
Who can?

Swunk and the Smoker's Lung

The New Jerusalem is irreverence
with Big Boy ready to serve you
on high holy days
Let mad dogs lie
at the shrine of shameless hucksterism

Red light district
teases the paying customers
as it dances
to hollowed body coolness

Green teeth smoked away
as the aliens wait to invade
Invites to Club Sixty-Nine
next to the bathrooms
Social media shills shrooms
Apathetic husbands wonder
when it all went wrong

Changes too much
but lost in the shuffle
It's so much easier to go back
to what your mind blows

High rollers stride across the room
while wine moms and Jack Daniels dads
meringue towards their seats
Air smells like foreboding rain

Fountainheads of human existence
search for art and imagination
Dogs and jackasses
dance burlesque to rave reviews
Music rests in the walls
for the rats to find redemption

When you relive
different versions
of the same scene
that's when it's time
to look for a new scene

And those who are salt and pepper
and punk as fuck
know the hard truth
That you either die a punk
or you live long enough
to see yourself
work at a microbrew

Drummers

There were four drummers playing
near a pavilion in the park
on my way to work
playing for no one
but themselves
on the first autumn day of the year.

So, like any self-respecting poet
I pulled out a poem and read aloud
to their beats
These drummers and I
performing for each other
A vagrant danced wildly in the wood
When it was over
we shared quarantine hugs
and I went to work
A few minutes late
but my boss never seemed
to notice

Red Eye Out of the Rat's Maze

Freshman fame makes assholes of us all
Even when we proclaim
to be the world's tallest short person
with the world's smallest big screen tv
Those who are up
still sweat and bleed the same
as those who are down

Bad decisions in hospice
gain the last sympathy
Convincing old friends
to go down rabbit holes
that will assuredly bite them
The money grabbers never bother
to learn who lives where
but always want to borrow
a little more
from Current Resident

Anna Karenina falls for the fighter
who screams
he will go to Valhalla
in a White Castle parking lot
after attracting the attentions
of every wannabe Wes Anderson wise ass
who could sing "These Days"

The last paisley ponytail
burns down his kingdom
unable to understand
it was him who lit the match
Who cries for his innocence
like many other Gen X progressives
who don't understand
where they lost the plot
like a computer
that runs on Windows 98
and still refuses all software updates

Man buns mansplain conflict mediation
from the second hand
to those in the middle of a fight
Never understanding
that a community
is never a building
but a people

The poets at the bar
make fun of those
who write of the moon
in verse
Those afraid of the third dimension
see Picasso's blue period
in the second
sitting with those
who spend lunch time on an empty stomach
because there is always something else
that needs attention

Fats cats went on a diet
and hid their money
but still flex power
when a dollar is on the line.
Feeling they can share
the hidden problems
they revel in
amongst their perceived kind

Trying to stay on course
past the beer drinkers and lotus eaters
who let the needle spin on the label
Scarlet skies make you look to the future
Though all the future ever is
is an old car
with a new coat of paint
The coasts that never gave your town
the time of day
tell you the rent is raised
as all the years you put in
don't mean a damn

Joe Buck bums a cigarette from Joe Camel
to bitch about the world not being like it once was
because everybody's talking
but no one can hear a word

Henry and Shane

I danced a jig
when I heard Henry Kissinger
had bit the big one
Hoping that if there was a Hell
he was right beside Nixon
getting everything he deserved
For Cambodia, Timor, Bangladesh, and Vietnam
For the assassinations he was tied to
So many laughed
as this 100 year old war criminal
finally parted ways
with this world

But in the wee hours of the next day
Shane MacGowan had passed
An Irish poet if ever there was one
who showed us
why you must get up on the stage
and let the world know what you mean
Outliving addiction
and succumbing to a virus
Those who knew of him
mourned
I raised a glass of Guinness
as many a pair of brown eyes
cried for Shane MacGowan

If You Believe That, I Got Some Land in Florida to Sell You

A regular at my favorite bar
tried to show me poetry
that they said was stolen from them
by a college professor
They said they wrote the poems
fifteen years ago
The copyright on the poems
was twenty-five years ago
They were only six months older
than me

April Anne

April Anne has a farm in upstate California
where hippie ideals meet hipster vibes
She watches as an ideal
turns to a forgotten idea
to a life she must leave

She dreams of high price lives of yesterday
when modern money could afford
a pauper's past
Visits to pipe dreams become more frequent
because it's all that she can afford

The older she gets
the more she realizes
that her teachers were right
She can get far in life
whenever she applies herself

Old friends knew she was smarter
and that's why she left
When a house becomes a home
it gets harder to leave
The beach is never
what the movies show it to be

The divorce came through in the mail
and it becomes another pile of paperwork
The crow's feet under her eyes
stare back at her

more than the rest of her
She thinks of those she never gave
an honest shot
and wonders if they could give her a chance
long after the good old days
have said good-bye

Rainbows

As I closed my eyes to the world
I saw colors
A rainbow taking all sorts of shapes
among the stars
All a message of love
A Wonderland on parade
minus the pink elephants

Feeling an ascension
with a brain stalling
like a car engine
At a loss for words
but words not needed
Seeing a glimpse of the edge
that has been said to be abandoned
Yet so many sojourn
to see if the leap is worth it

Love pulled me from beyond
and as I opened my eyes
I stared at my ceiling
awake with nothing
while memoirs of past jumps
played on my phone

Ain't It Just Like Norman Fucking Rockwell

Mythology lies in music
as Jagger and Bowie
fornicate in our minds
before dancing in the street
as too many rock stars
are said to have their stomachs pumped
for swallowing too much cum
as Sid and Nancy
are held as relationship goals
by those who have never been loved

American Pie tells many tales
and leaves no solution
Makes sense to those
who were also lost in space
The wild west is for those who think
they'd actually survive it
only to get gut shot
for shits and giggles

Russian writers are for the intellectuals
who humble brag their intelligence
German philosophers are for those
who know they know more
Greek mythology it for the hipster
who knows it's pronounces Herakles

The boys from the front
dance the foxtrot to nursery crymes
as Washington crosses the Delaware
hoping to avoid T. S. Eliot
and death by water
They call to the jolly flatboat men in port
to help them reach shore
but all are too drunk to pay attention
and barges drift
with the turning tide

Jacob sleeps on the bench
tired of climbing the ladder
and a bit scared
after seeing poor Tim Finnegan
take a fall
though rumor was
he was drunk when he climbed

Dogs cry for equal rights
when learning they only count
as half a person
in the American home
I guess that's what loyalty gets you

Tom and Jack and Neil and Allen
look for the heart of Saturday
with only Tom not yet a ghost
but still clanging his chains together
like he is one
because he likes the sound
with others following their sojourn

True love exists for those
who will never buy a home together
Dreams are the side quests
with the main objective
always being able to learn to swim

Bob singing another never-ending verse
of "Desolation Row"
while the typewriters crank out
page 1200
of the Great American Novel
while Fitzgerald did it all
within 180
As the young guitarist
tries to play Van Halen
Lou tells the kid
all they need
is three chords and an attitude

Americana takes the Constitution
but forgets Magna Carta
Takes Jesus
but leaves Judaism
Takes the right to bear arms
but leaves separation of Church and State
If England was sold by the pound
then I wish "dollar"
was also a system of weight measurement
so one can say the same
of the United States

Memo to Turner

Isn't it a pity
That no one knows what it takes
for the final straw to break
I wonder if this is what
John and Paul felt
when 1970 hit them
like a ton of bricks

Criticism is damned if it does
and damned if it doesn't
Generalities are met
with demand for examples
Examples are claimed
to be petty
But what is petty to one
is relevant to the other
with one or two isolated incidents
but many a pattern
The responsibilities never appreciated
when never dealt with
One raised voice
leads to another
and words that can never
be taken back

Questions asked but never answered
Love stated but never heard
The culmination of so much
when things get too big
can two people ever comprehend it all

When anger subsides and all that is left
is the wreckage
Will one feel the same as the other
when there is only warm tears,
a hand that won't stop shaking,
and sharp pains in the chest
because anger does its worst
when it's allowed to play the waiting game

A decade is long enough to know the other
at their best and worst
No hero or villain in any of these stories
Now the one who was always in your corner
stands across the ring
With both of you believing you're right
and willing to fight
for what you believe in
No happy endings
with these kinds of tales
just red flags
people are sure
will never happen to them

Boredom Comes for the Best of Us

The fallen snow
holds just as much appeal
to me
as the sexy shapes of cigarette smoke
before it disappears
The warmth that the body feels
drinking coffee or tea
on a winter's day
when you're too cheap to put the heat on

The booze is down the drain
but I'm sure it will be in me again
before too long
I still live for high days
I just take better care
not to shit where I eat

A friend asked me
why he doesn't see me
out at the bars
as much anymore
I told him
because you never buy booze
you just rent it

The Children of Marx and Coca-Cola

Finding love
like a Godard film
is a wonderful feeling
but impractical in the real world

What will the lady see
in the depths of her night
Too much time on the mind
frustrates the idle hands
of her calico skies

Tough fronts mean nothing
without something to back it up
Never declare what you know
will be thrown out

Put two geniuses together
and you'll find two idiots
High on the rooftop
the day takes all day long

One hundred memorable moments today
that will be forgotten tomorrow
But the memory of a face
will last a lifetime

Banshee

Another unsatisfied customer
from the AT&T store across the street
took the sandwich board they had
to stand in the middle of traffic
and scream
about how AT&T had ripped her off
Promising a deal
but charging her twice the usual amount
due to a fine print
she was told she didn't need to read

The store clerks hid
as they called the cops
popping their heads up for a moment
to point and laugh
at the situation they knew they caused

No one wants to be the person
who reaches their limit
but still we all hit it
because the world is a villain
and we are all heroes
or anti-heroes

When the cops came
they escorted her off the street
and listened to her
But her rage was too much by that point
She screamed her stress to the window

as loud as she could
loud enough to be heard
by a five block radius

When she was done
she wiped away her tears
and sat on the nearby bench
crying as she told the police
that she had no money
and no phone
because of the fine print
she was told she didn't need to read

As the cops walked her to her car
she lamented that she didn't know
if she had enough gas
to get home
The officer who had been listening to her
slipped her forty bucks

The lady went on her way
with forty bucks to get her by
however long that could carry her
while the clerks pointed and laughed
as another customer came into the store
to be told that they shouldn't worry
about the fine print
they didn't need to read.

What Would Harry Dean Say?

(A Poem for Jason Ryberg)

Money for books
becomes betting on a happy ending
Hands fidgety
because they want to fix
another problem
beyond their reach

Last time I saw you,
you declared that Jerry Reed
was either the James Brown of country
or the Foghorn Leghorn of funk

I asked a universe
I was already indebted to
for a big favor
but it helped
that I wasn't
the only one asking

You ain't done yet, Baron
There's still more to do
Come on home
Your friends await
your return

Take a Piece, But Not Too Much

Starting the day
by searching for the latest doom and gloom
on your phone
Checking if the water is fit to drink
If the air is fit to breathe
How many were killed
in the latest school shooting
or the latest bombing
Were any rights voted out of law
What union is on strike today
Are the buses actually running on time today
Flashbacks of failures
you've been drilled to never forget

And still we press on
boats against the currents
As the ones who gave us this present
die in their greed
regretting they didn't have more
And wondering why our poems
aren't a little more positive
We still go on
ready to change with the world
because while failure is inevitable
we will still succeed
where we can

Hanging with the Illegitimate Brats
of Andrew Dice Clay

I'd respect these spoiled fuckers
if they weren't getting drunk and fighting
due to Mango Smirnoff Ice
Making the fucktard's journey
to a Snoop Dogg show
that makes my old man energy scream,
"Y'all don't know shit
about 'Nuthin' But a G Thang'!"

If this were twenty years ago,
every last one of these spoiled shits
would be on a Girls Gone Wild advert
at two in the morning
Showing enough to make you want to jerk off
but never showing enough
to make it worthwhile

End of the Tour

I don't wanna say goodbye
to my friends
I want to see them everyday
I want us all
to live in one of those Italian villages
that have been deserted for years
and that they're begging people
to move to

Where I know I'm understood
and an informed member of society
Where I'm not just the weirdo
who writes shit
At least not the only one

Where hugs will always mean
I love you
and empathy is paramount
Instead we are all spread
across the globe
for reunions to mean the world
There's never enough time
but we make the most anyway
because it's all we have

Daniel W. Wright is a poet, editor, and fiction writer. He is the co-founder of Back of the Class Press. Wright most recently released the novella, *Snake Oil* (Dark Heart Press, 2024). He is the author of five full-length collections of poetry, two works of fiction, and co-author of two poetry splits. His work has appeared in numerous print and online journals. Wright currently resides in St. Louis, MO, where you can usually find him in a bar or a bookstore.

This project was made possible, in part, by generous support from the Osage Arts Community.

Osage Arts Community provides temporary time, space and support for the creation of new artistic works in a retreat format, serving creative people of all kinds — visual artists, composers, poets, fiction and nonfiction writers. Located on a 152-acre farm in an isolated rural mountainside setting in Central Missouri and bordered by ¾ of a mile of the Gasconade River, OAC provides residencies to those working alone, as well as welcoming collaborative teams, offering living space and workspace in a country environment to emerging and mid-career artists. For more information, visit us at www.osageac.org

Osage Arts Community